The Tale of the Story-Wise Icelander

Original Text, Translations, and Word Lists

Translated by Matthew Leigh Embleton

Copyright ©2025 Matthew Leigh Embleton. All rights reserved.

The Tale of the Story-Wise Icelander

The Tale of the Story-Wise Icelander (*Old Norse*) 4
Word List *(Old Norse to English)*..7
Word List *(English to Old Norse)* 11
The Tale of the Story-Wise Icelander (*Old Icelandic*) 15
Word List *(Old Icelandic to English)*...18
Word List *(English to Old Icelandic)*...22
A Word Comparison of Old Norse and Old Icelandic Words 26

Cover: Old Norse text over an outline of Iceland. Author's design.

The original Old Norse and Old Icelandic texts are in the public domain.
These translations ©2022 Matthew Leigh Embleton
©2025 Matthew Leigh Embleton (This Edition)

Acknowledgments

I have long been fascinated by languages and history, and I am very grateful to the special people in my life who have supported and encouraged me in my work. Thank you for believing in me. You know who you are.

Introduction

Old Norse is a North Germanic language spoken by inhabitants of Scandinavia from about the 7th to the 15th centuries. Old Icelandic is a variety of Old West Norse that emerged during the Norse settlement of Iceland in the second half of the 9th century. The rich tradition of Icelandic literature survived by oral tradition over several centuries before being written down in the 13th Century. The Tale of the Story-Wise Icelander (*Íslendings þáttr sögufróða*) is one of the many Tales of Icelanders or *Íslendingaþættir*. The word '*þáttr*' (plural: '*þættir*') translates as a strand of rope or a yarn, comparable to the word 'yarn' in English sometimes used to refer to a story.

This book contains:
- The Tale of the Story-Wise Icelander (Íslendings þáttr sögufróða) (Old Norse Version)
- An Old Norse to English Word List
- An English to Old Norse Word List
- The Tale of the Story-Wise Icelander (Íslendings þáttr sögufróða) (Old Icelandic Version)
- An Old Icelandic to English Word List
- An English to Old Icelandic Word List
- A Word Comparison of Old Norse and Old Icelandic words

The texts are presented in their original form, with a literal word-for-word line-by-line translation, and a Modern English translation, all side-by-side. In this way, it is possible to see and feel how the worked and how it has evolved. This book is designed to be of use and interest to anyone with a passion for the Old Norse or Old Icelandic language, Norse history, or languages and history in general.

The Tale of the Story-Wise Icelander (Old Norse)

The Tale of the Story-Wise Icelander (*Old Norse*)

Old Norse	Literal	English
Svá barst at eitthvert sumar, at einn íslenzkr maðr, ungr ok fráligr, kom til [Haralds] konungs ok bað hann ásjá.	So bore to one summer, that one Icelander man, young and bright, came to [Harald's] the-king and bid him assistance.	So it happened one summer that an Icelander man, young and bright, came to the king and asked for his assistance.
Konungr spurði, ef hann kynni nökkura fræði, en hann lézt kunna sögur.	The-king asked, if he knew-of any wisdom, that he let could say.	The king asked if he knew of any lore that he could tell stories.
Þá sagði konungr, at hann mun [taka] við honum, en hann skal þess skyldr at skemmta ávallt, er vildi, hverrgi sem hann bæði.	Then said the-king, that he would [take] with him, but he shall this should to entertain always, as willed, each who he bid.	Then the king said that he would keep him but he should always entertain anyone who asked him.
Ok svá gerir hann, ok er hann vinsæll við hirðina, ok gefa þeir honum klæði, ok konungr gefr honum vápn í hönd sér,	And so did he, and was he popular with king's-men, and gave they to-him clothes, and the-king gave him weapons in hand for-him,	And so he did, and he was popular with the king's men, and they gave him clothes and the king gave him weapons in his hand.
ok líðr nú svá fram til jóla.	and Passed now so from until Yule.	And so it passed until yule.
Þá ógleðr Íslending, ok spyrr konungr, hví þat gegndi.	Then un-glad Icelander, and asked the-king, what the reason.	Then the Icelander grew sad and the king asked what the reason was.
Hann kvað mislyndi sína til koma.	He said mood his towards came.	He said that this was a bad mood that had come on.
Ekki mun þat vera, segir konungr, "ok mun ek geta til.	Not could that be, said the-king, "and could I guess to.	"That could not be", said the king, "and I shall guess what it is.
Þess get ek til", segir hann, "at nú muni uppi sögur þínar.	This guess I to", said he, "that now recalled up stories yours.	This is my guess", he said, "that all the stories you remember you have now told.
Þú hefir ávallt skemmt í vetr, hverjum sem beiðzt hefir.	You have always entertained about winter, everyone who bid has.	You have always entertained this winter everyone who has asked you.
Mun þér nú illt þykkja, at þrjóti at jólunum".	Could you now ill valued, as-a failure this Yule".	Shall you now feel bad about yule".

The Tale of the Story-Wise Icelander (Old Norse)

Old Norse	Literal	English
Jafnt er svá sem þú getr, segir hann. "Ein er sagan eftir, ok þori ek þá eigi hér at segja, því at þat er útferðarsaga þín".	Equal is so as you guess, said he. "One of the-saga remaining, and dare I this not here to say, because that this is out-faring-saga yours".	"It is equal to your guess", he said, "one of the sagas is remaining and I dare not tell this here, because this is the saga of your travels".
Konungr mælti:	The-king spoke:	The king said:
Sú er ok svá sagan, at mér er mest um at heyra, ok skaltu nú ekki skemmta til jólanna fram, er menn eru nú í starfi,	So is also such saga, that to-me is most about to hear, and shall-you now none entertain until Yule forwards, as the-men are now to work,	"So it is the saga that I most want to hear, and you shall now not entertain anyone until yule, as the men are now busy with work.
en jóladag skaltu til taka þessar sögu ok segja af nökkurn spöl, ok ek mun svá til stilla með þér, at jafndrjúg mun verða sagan ok jólin.	but Yule-day shall-you to take this saga and say of something short, and I shall so to still with to-you, that equal-long shall be said also Yule.	But on the day of yule, take to this saga and tell a short amount of it, and I shall arrange it with you that the saga will be as long as yule.
Nú eru drykkjur miklar of jólin, ok má skömmum við sitja at hlýða skemmtan, ok ekki muntu á finna, meðan þú segir, hvárt mér þykkir vel eða illa.	Now they-are drinking much about Yule, and may-be short with sitting and listening-to entertainment, and not shall to find, while you say, whether I think well or ill.	Now they are drinking a lot at yule and they may have little time to sit and listen to stories, and you shall not be able to see whether I think I am pleased or not".
Nú er þat ok, at Íslendingr segir söguna, hefr upp jóladag ok segir of hríð, ok biðr konungr brátt hætta.	Now was it and, the Icelander said the-saga, had upped Yule-day and said of awhile, and asked the-king soon concluded.	Now it was and the Icelander told the saga, he began on the day of yule and spoke a while but the king soon asked him to stop.
Taka menn at drekka, ok ræða margir um, at þó sé djörfung í þessu, er hann Íslendingr segir þessa sögu, eða hversu konungi muni virðast.	Took men to drinking, and discussed many about, that though his boldness in this, that he The-Icelander said this saga, or how-so the-king would worth.	The men took to drinking and many discussed how bold it was of the Icelander to tell this saga, or how the king would value it.
Sumum þykkir hann vel segja, en sumir vinnast minna at.	Some thought he well said, but some won less of.	Some of them thought the saga went well but some valued it less.
Ferr svá fram of jólin.	Went so forwards about Yule.	And so it went during yule.
Konungr var vandr at, at hlýtt væri vel, ok stenzt þat á með umstilli konungs, er lokit er sögunni ok jólin þrýtr.	The-king was particularly that, to listen should-be well, and stood it about with about-guidance the-king's, was ended the saga and Yule ended.	The king was particular that it should be listened to well and with the king's guidance the saga ended and yule ended together.

The Tale of the Story-Wise Icelander (Old Norse)

Old Norse	Literal	English
Ok it þrettánda kveld, er lokit var sögunni áðr of daginn, mælti konungr:	And the thirteenth evening, when ended was the-saga earlier of the-day, spoke the-king:	At the thirteenth evening after the saga was told, the king spoke:
Er þér eigi forvitni á, Íslendingr, segir hann, "hversu mér líkar sagan?"	Are you not for-knowing about, Icelander, said he, "how-so to-me liked the-saga?"	"Are you curious, Icelander", he said, "how I liked the saga?"
Hræddr em ek um, herra, segir hann.	Scared am I about, lord, said he.	"I am scared to know, my lord", he said.
Konungr mælti:	The-king spoke:	The king spoke:
Mér þykkir allvel, ok hvergi verr en efni eru til, eða hverr kenndi þér söguna?	I thought all-well, and neither worse than the-matter was to, but who taught you the-saga?	"I thought it was all good and no worse than the matter was, but who taught you the saga?"
Hann svarar:	He answered:	He answered:
Þat var vanði minn út á landinu, at ek fór hvert sumar til þings, ok namk hvert sumar af sögunni nökkut at Halldóri Snorrasyni.	It was custom mine out-in the country, that I travelled each summer to assembly, and took each summer of saga something from Halldor Snorrason.	"It was my habit out in my country that I travelled each summer to the assembly, and I learned each summer something of the saga from Halldor Snorrason".
Þá er eigi kynligt, segir konungr, "at þú kunnir vel, ok mun þér at gæfu verða, ok ver með mér velkominn, ok skal þat heimilt ávallt, er þú vill".	Then is not extraordinary, said the-king, "that you know well, and shall to-you of gifted be, and be with me welcome, and shall it allow all-full, as you wish".	"Then it is no wonder", said the king, "that you know it well, and you shall be gifted and welcome with me and I shall grant you as you wish".
Konungr fekk honum góðan kaupeyri, ok varð hann þroskamaðr.	The-king gave him good wares, and was he vigorous-man.	The king gave him good wares and he was a vigorous man.

Word List *(Old Norse to English)*

Old Norse	English

A, a

af	of
allvel	all-well
at	and, as-a, from, of, that, the, this, to

Á, á

á	about, the, to
áðr	earlier
ásjá	assistance
ávallt	all-full, always

B, b

bað	bid
bæði	bid
barst	bore
beiðzt	bid
biðr	asked
brátt	soon

D, d

daginn	the-day
djörfung	boldness
drekka	drinking
drykkjur	drinking

E, e

eða	but, or
ef	if
efni	the-matter
eftir	remaining
eigi	not
Ein	one
einn	one
eitthvert	one
ek	I
ekki	none, not
em	am
en	but, than, that
Er	are, as, is, of, that, the, was, when
eru	are, they-are, was

F, f

fekk	gave
Ferr	went
finna	find
fór	travelled
forvitni	for-knowing
fræði	wisdom
fráligr	bright
fram	forwards, from

G, g

gæfu	gifted
gefa	gave
gefr	gave
gegndi	reason
gerir	did
get	guess
geta	guess
getr	guess
góðan	good

H, h

hætta	concluded
Halldóri	Halldor (name)
hann	he, him
Haralds	Harald's (name)
hefir	has, have
hefr	had

Word List (Old Norse to English)

Old Norse	English
heimilt	allow
hér	here
herra	lord
heyra	hear
hirðina	king's-men
hlýða	listening-to
hlýtt	listen
hönd	hand
honum	him, to-him
Hræddr	scared
hríð	awhile
hvárt	whether
hvergi	neither
hverjum	everyone
hverr	who
hverrgi	each
hversu	how-so
hvert	each
hví	what

I, i

Old Norse	English
líðr	passed
illa	ill
illt	ill
it	the

Í, í

Old Norse	English
í	about, in, to
Íslending	Icelander
Íslendingr	Icelander, the-Icelander
íslenzkr	Icelander

J, j

Old Norse	English
jafndrjúg	equal-long
Jafnt	equal
jóla	Yule
jóladag	Yule-day
jólanna	Yule
jólin	Yule
jólunum	Yule

K, k

Old Norse	English
kaupeyri	wares
kenndi	taught
klæði	clothes
kom	came
koma	came
konungi	the-king
Konungr	the-king
konungs	the-king, the-king's
kunna	could
kunnir	know
kvað	said
kveld	evening
kynligt	extraordinary
kynni	knew-of

L, l

Old Norse	English
landinu	country
lézt	let
líkar	liked
lokit	ended

M, m

Old Norse	English
má	may-be
maðr	man
mælti	spoke
margir	many
með	with
meðan	while
menn	men, the-men
mér	I, me, to-me
mest	most
miklar	much
minn	mine
minna	less
mislyndi	mood
mun	could, shall, would
muni	recalled, would

Word List (Old Norse to English)

Old Norse	English
muntu	shall

N, n

Old Norse	English
namk	took
nökkura	any
nökkurn	something
nökkut	something
nú	now

O, o

Old Norse	English
of	about, of
ok	also, and

Ó, ó

Old Norse	English
ógleðr	un-glad

R, r

Old Norse	English
ræða	discussed

S, s

Old Norse	English
sagan	saga, said, the-saga
sagði	said
sé	his
segir	said, say
segja	said, say
sem	as, who
sér	for-him
sína	his
sitja	sitting
skal	shall
skaltu	shall-you
skemmt	entertained
skemmta	entertain
skemmtan	entertainment
skömmum	short
skyldr	should
Snorrasyni	Snorrason (name)
sögu	saga
söguna	the-saga
sögunni	saga, the-saga
sögur	say, stories
spöl	short
spurði	asked
spyrr	asked
starfi	work
stenzt	stood
stilla	still
Sú	so
sumar	summer
sumir	some
Sumum	some
svá	so, such
svarar	answered

T, t

Old Norse	English
taka	take, took
til	to, towards, until

Þ, þ

Old Norse	English
Þá	then, this
þat	it, that, the, this
þeir	they
þér	to-you, you
þess	this
þessa	this
þessar	this
þessu	this
þín	yours
þínar	yours
þings	assembly
þó	though
þori	dare
þrettánda	thirteenth
þrjóti	failure
þroskamaðr	vigorous-man
þrýtr	ended
Þú	you
því	because

Word List (Old Norse to English)

Old Norse	English
þykkir	think, thought
þykkja	valued

U, u

um	about
umstilli	about-guidance
ungr	young
upp	upped
uppi	up

Ú, ú

út	out-in
útferðarsaga	out-faring-saga

V, v

væri	should-be
vanði	custom
vandr	particularly
vápn	weapons
var	was
varð	was
vel	well
velkominn	welcome
ver	be
vera	be
verða	be
verr	worse
vetr	winter
við	with
vildi	willed
vill	wish
vinnast	won
vinsæll	popular
virðast	worth

Word List *(English to Old Norse)*

English	*Old Norse*

A, a

about	*á, í, of, um*
about-guidance	*umstilli*
all-full	*ávallt*
allow	*heimilt*
all-well	*allvel*
also	*ok*
always	*ávallt*
am	*em*
and	*at, ok*
answered	*svarar*
any	*nökkura*
are	*Er, eru*
as	*er, sem*
as-a	*at*
asked	*biðr, spurði, spyrr*
assembly	*þings*
assistance	*ásjá*
awhile	*hríð*

B, b

be	*ver, vera, verða*
because	*því*
bid	*bað, bæði, beiðzt*
boldness	*djörfung*
bore	*barst*
bright	*fráligr*
but	*eða, en*

C, c

came	*kom, koma*
clothes	*klæði*
concluded	*hætta*
could	*kunna, mun*
country	*landinu*
custom	*vanði*

D, d

dare	*þori*
did	*gerir*
discussed	*ræða*
drinking	*drekka, drykkjur*

E, e

each	*hverrgi, hvert*
earlier	*áðr*
ended	*lokit, þrýtr*
entertain	*skemmta*
entertained	*skemmt*
entertainment	*skemmtan*
equal	*Jafnt*
equal-long	*jafndrjúg*
evening	*kveld*
everyone	*hverjum*
extraordinary	*kynligt*

F, f

failure	*þrjóti*
find	*finna*
for-him	*sér*
for-knowing	*forvitni*
forwards	*fram*
from	*at, fram*

G, g

gave	*fekk, gefa, gefr*
gifted	*gæfu*
good	*góðan*
guess	*get, geta, getr*

Word List (English to Old Norse)

English	*Old Norse*

H, h

had	*hefr*
Halldor (name)	*Halldóri*
hand	*hönd*
Harald's (name)	*Haralds*
has	*hefir*
have	*hefir*
he	*hann*
hear	*heyra*
here	*hér*
him	*hann, honum*
his	*sé, sína*
how-so	*hversu*

I, i

I	*ek, mér*
Icelander	*Íslending, Íslendingr, íslenzkr*
if	*ef*
ill	*illa, illt*
in	*í*
is	*er*
it	*þat*

K, k

king's-men	*hirðina*
knew-of	*kynni*
know	*kunnir*

L, l

less	*minna*
let	*lézt*
liked	*líkar*
listen	*hlýtt*
listening-to	*hlýða*
lord	*herra*

M, m

man	*maðr*
many	*margir*
may-be	*má*
me	*mér*
men	*menn*
mine	*minn*
mood	*mislyndi*
most	*mest*
much	*miklar*

N, n

neither	*hvergi*
none	*ekki*
not	*eigi, Ekki*
now	*nú*

O, o

of	*af, at, er, of*
one	*Ein, einn, eitthvert*
or	*eða*
out-faring-saga	*útferðarsaga*
out-in	*út*

P, p

particularly	*vandr*
passed	*líðr*
popular	*vinsæll*

R, r

reason	*gegndi*
recalled	*muni*
remaining	*eftir*

Word List (English to Old Norse)

English	*Old Norse*	English	*Old Norse*
		think	*þykkir*
		thirteenth	*þrettánda*
		this	*at, þá, þat, þess, þessa, þessar, þessu*
		though	*þó*

S, s

English	*Old Norse*
saga	*sagan, sögu, sögunni*
said	*kvað, sagan, sagði, segir, segja*
say	*segir, segja, sögur*
scared	*Hræddr*
shall	*mun, muntu, skal*
shall-you	*skaltu*
short	*skömmum, spöl*
should	*skyldr*
should-be	*væri*
sitting	*sitja*
Snorrason (name)	*Snorrasyni*
so	*Sú, svá*
some	*sumir, Sumum*
something	*nökkurn, nökkut*
soon	*brátt*
spoke	*mælti*
still	*stilla*
stood	*stenzt*
stories	*sögur*
such	*svá*
summer	*sumar*

English	*Old Norse*
thought	*þykkir*
to	*á, at, í, til*
to-him	*honum*
to-me	*mér*
took	*namk, Taka*
towards	*til*
to-you	*þér*
travelled	*fór*

U, u

English	*Old Norse*
un-glad	*ógleðr*
until	*til*
up	*uppi*
upped	*upp*

V, v

English	*Old Norse*
valued	*þykkja*
vigorous-man	*þroskamaðr*

T, t

English	*Old Norse*
take	*taka*
taught	*kenndi*
than	*en*
that	*at, en, er, þat*
the	*á, at, er, it, þat*
the-day	*daginn*
the-Icelander	*Íslendingr*
the-king	*konungi, Konungr, konungs*
the-king's	*konungs*
the-matter	*efni*
the-men	*menn*
then	*Þá*
the-saga	*sagan, söguna, sögunni*
they	*þeir*
they-are	*eru*

W, w

English	*Old Norse*
wares	*kaupeyri*
was	*er, eru, var, varð*
weapons	*vápn*
welcome	*velkominn*
well	*vel*
went	*Ferr*
what	*hví*
when	*er*
whether	*hvárt*
while	*meðan*
who	*hverr, sem*
willed	*vildi*
winter	*vetr*
wisdom	*fræði*
wish	*vill*

Word List (English to Old Norse)

English	Old Norse
with	*með, við*
won	*vinnast*
work	*starfi*
worse	*verr*
worth	*virðast*
would	*mun, muni*

Y, y

you	*þér, Þú*
young	*ungr*
yours	*þín, þínar*
Yule	*jóla, jólanna, jólin, jólunum*
Yule-day	*jóladag*

The Tale of the Story-Wise Icelander (*Old Icelandic*)

Old Icelandic	Literal	English
Svo barst að eitthvert sumar að einn íslenskur maður, ungur og frálegur, kom til konungs og bað hann ásjá.	So bore to one summer that one Icelander man, young and bright, came to the-king and bid him assistance.	So it happened one summer that an Icelander man, young and bright, came to the king and asked for his assistance.
Konungur spurði ef hann kynni nokkverja fræði en hann lést kunna sögur.	The-king asked if he knew-of any wisdom that he let could say.	The king asked if he knew of any lore that he could tell stories.
Þá sagði konungur að hann mun taka við honum en hann skal þess skyldur að skemmta ávallt er vildi, hvergi sem hann bæði.	Then said the-king that he would take with him but he shall this should to entertain always as willed, each who he bid-(asked).	Then the king said that he would keep him but he should always entertain anyone who asked him.
Og svo gerir hann og er hann vinsæll við hirðina og gefa þeir honum klæði og konungur gefur honum vopn í hönd sér.	And so did he and was he popular with king's-men and gave they to-him clothes and the-king gave him weapons in hand for-him.	And so he did, and he was popular with the king's men, and they gave him clothes and the king gave him weapons in his hand.
Og líður nú svo fram til jóla.	And passed now so from until yule.	And so it passed until yule.
Þá ógleður Íslending og spyr konungur hví það gegndi.	Then un-glad-(sad) Icelander and asked the-king what the reason.	Then the Icelander grew sad and the king asked what the reason was.
Hann kvað mislyndi sína til koma.	He said mood his towards came.	He said that this was a bad mood that had come on.
"Ekki mun það vera", segir konungur, "og mun eg geta til.	"Not could that be", said the-king, "and could I guess to.	"That could not be", said the king, "and I shall guess what it is.
Þess get eg til", segir hann, "að nú muni uppi sögur þínar.	This guess I to", said he, "that now recalled up stories yours.	This is my guess", he said, "that all the stories you remember you have now told.
Þú hefir ávallt skemmt í vetur hverjum sem beiðst hefir.	You have always entertained about winter everyone who bid-(asked) has.	You have always entertained this winter everyone who has asked you.
Mun þér nú illt þykja að þrjóti að jólunum".	Could you now ill valued as-a failure this yule".	Shall you now feel bad about yule".

The Tale of the Story-Wise Icelander (Old Icelandic)

Old Icelandic	Literal	English
"Jafnt er svo sem þú getur", segir hann, "ein er sagan eftir og þori ég þá eigi hér að segja því að það er útferðarsaga þín".	"Equal is so as you guess", said he, "one of the-saga remaining and dare I this not here to say because that this is out-faring-saga yours".	"It is equal to your guess", he said, "one of the sagas is remaining and I dare not tell this here, because this is the saga of your travels".
Konungur mælti:	The-king spoke:	The king said:
"Sú er og svo sagan að mér er mest um að heyra og skaltu nú ekki skemmta til jólanna fram er menn eru nú í starfi.	"So is also such saga that to-me is most about to hear and shall-you now none entertain until yule forwards as the-men are now to work.	"So it is the saga that I most want to hear, and you shall now not entertain anyone until yule, as the men are now busy with work.
En jóladag skaltu til taka þessa sögu og segja af nokkvern spöl og ég mun svo til stilla með þér að jafndrjúg mun verða sagan og jólin.	But yule-day shall-you to take this saga and say of something short and I shall so to still with to-you that equal-long shall be said also yule.	But on the day of yule, take to this saga and tell a short amount of it, and I shall arrange it with you that the saga will be as long as yule.
Nú eru drykkjur miklar of jólin og má skömmum við sitja að hlýða skemmtan og ekki muntu á finna meðan þú segir hvort mér þykir vel eða illa".	Now they-are drinking much about yule and may-be short with sitting and listening-to entertainment and not shall to find while you say whether I think well or ill".	Now they are drinking a lot at yule and they may have little time to sit and listen to stories, and you shall not be able to see whether I think I am pleased or not".
Nú er það og að Íslendingur segir söguna, hefur upp jóladag og segir of hríð og biður konungur brátt hætta.	Now was it and the Icelander said the-saga, had upped yule-day and said of awhile and asked the-king soon concluded.	Now it was and the Icelander told the saga, he began on the day of yule and spoke a while but the king soon asked him to stop.
Taka menn að drekka og ræða margir um að þó sé djörfung í þessu er hann Íslendingur segir þessa sögu eða hversu konungi muni virðast.	Took men to drinking and discussed many about that though his boldness in this that he The-Icelander said this saga or how-so the-king would worth-(value).	The men took to drinking and many discussed how bold it was of the Icelander to tell this saga, or how the king would value it.
Sumum þykir hann vel segja en sumir vinnast minna að.	Some thought he well said but some won less of.	Some of them thought the saga went well but some valued it less.
Fer svo fram of jólin.	Went so forwards about yule.	And so it went during yule.

The Tale of the Story-Wise Icelander (Old Icelandic)

Old Icelandic	Literal	English
Konungur var vandur að að hlýtt væri vel og stenst það á með umstilli konungs er lokið er sögunni og jólin þrýtur.	The-king was particularly that to listen should-be well and stood it about with about-guidance the-king's was ended the saga and yule ended.	The king was particular that it should be listened to well and with the king's guidance the saga ended and yule ended together.
Og hið þrettánda kveld er lokið var sögunni áður of daginn mælti konungur:	And the thirteenth evening when ended was the-saga earlier of the-day spoke the-king:	At the thirteenth evening after the saga was told, the king spoke:
"Er þér eigi forvitni á Íslendingur", segir hann, "hversu mér líkar sagan?".	"Are you not for-knowing-(curious) about Icelander", said he, "how-so to-me liked the-saga?"	"Are you curious, Icelander", he said, "how I liked the saga?"
"Hræddur em eg um herra", segir hann.	"Scared am I about lord", said he.	"I am scared to know, my lord", he said.
Konungur mælti:	The-king spoke:	The king spoke:
"Mér þykir allvel og hvergi verr en efni eru til eða hver kenndi þér söguna?".	"I thought all-well and neither worse than the-matter was to but who taught you the-saga?"	"I thought it was all good and no worse than the matter was, but who taught you the saga?"
Hann svarar:	He answered:	He answered:
"Það var vandi minn út á landinu að eg fór hvert sumar til þings og nam eg hvert sumar af sögunni nakkvað að Halldóri Snorrasyni".	"It was custom mine out-in the country that I travelled each summer to assembly and took I each summer of saga something from Halldor Snorrason".	"It was my habit out in my country that I travelled each summer to the assembly, and I learned each summer something of the saga from Halldor Snorrason".
"Þá er eigi kynlegt", segir konungur, "að þú kunnir vel og mun þér að gæfu verða og ver með mér velkominn og skal það heimilt ávallt er þú vilt.	"Then is not extraordinary", said the-king, "that you know well and shall to-you of gifted be and be with me welcome and shall it allow all-full as you wish.	"Then it is no wonder", said the king, "that you know it well, and you shall be gifted and welcome with me and I shall grant you as you wish".
Konungur fékk honum góðan kaupeyri og varð hann þroskamaður.	The-king gave him good wares and was he vigorous-man.	The king gave him good wares and he was a vigorous man.

Word List *(Old Icelandic to English)*

Old Icelandic	English

A, a

að	and, as-a, from, of, that, the, this, to
af	of
allvel	all-well

Á, á

á	about, the, to
áður	earlier
ásjá	assistance
ávallt	all-full, always

B, b

bað	bid
bæði	bid
barst	bore
beiðst	bid
biður	asked
brátt	soon

D, d

daginn	the-day
djörfung	boldness
drekka	drinking
drykkjur	drinking

E, e

eða	but, or
ef	if
efni	the-matter
eftir	remaining
eg	I
eigi	not
ein	one
einn	one
eitthvert	one
ekki	none, not
em	am
en	but, than, that
er	are, as, is, of, that, the, was, when
eru	are, they-are, was

F, f

fékk	gave
fer	went
finna	find
fór	travelled
forvitni	for-knowing
fræði	wisdom
frálegur	bright
fram	forwards, from

G, g

gæfu	gifted
gefa	gave
gefur	gave
gegndi	reason
gerir	did
get	guess
geta	guess
getur	guess
góðan	good

H, h

hætta	concluded
halldóri	Halldor (name)
hann	he, him
hefir	has, have
hefur	had
heimilt	allow

Word List (Old Icelandic to English)

Old Icelandic	English
hér	here
herra	lord
heyra	hear
hið	the
hirðina	king's-men
hlýða	listening-to
hlýtt	listen
hönd	hand
honum	him, to-him
hræddur	scared
hríð	awhile
hver	who
hvergi	each, neither
hverjum	everyone
hversu	how-so
hvert	each
hví	what
hvort	whether

I, i

illa	ill
illt	ill

Í, í

í	about, in, to
íslending	Icelander
íslendingur	Icelander, the-Icelander
íslenskur	Icelander

J, j

jafndrjúg	equal-long
jafnt	equal
jóla	yule
jóladag	yule-day
jólanna	yule
jólin	yule
jólunum	yule

K, k

Old Icelandic	English
kaupeyri	wares
kenndi	taught
klæði	clothes
kom	came
koma	came
konungi	the-king
konungs	the-king, the-king's
konungur	the-king
kunna	could
kunnir	know
kvað	said
kveld	evening
kynlegt	extraordinary
kynni	knew-of

L, l

landinu	country
lést	let
líður	passed
líkar	liked
lokið	ended

M, m

má	may-be
maður	man
mælti	spoke
margir	many
með	with
meðan	while
menn	men, the-men
mér	I, me, to-me
mest	most
miklar	much
minn	mine
minna	less
mislyndi	mood
mun	could, shall, would
muni	recalled, would
muntu	shall

Word List (Old Icelandic to English)

Old Icelandic	English

N, n

nakkvað	something
nam	took
nokkverja	any
nokkvern	something
nú	now

O, o

of	about, of
og	also, and

Ó, ó

ógleður	un-glad

R, r

ræða	discussed

S, s

sagan	saga, said, the-saga
sagði	said
sé	his
segir	said, say
segja	said, say
sem	as, who
sér	for-him
sína	his
sitja	sitting
skal	shall
skaltu	shall-you
skemmt	entertained
skemmta	entertain
skemmtan	entertainment
skömmum	short
skyldur	should
snorrasyni	Snorrason (name)
sögu	saga
söguna	the-saga
sögunni	saga, the-saga
sögur	say, stories
spöl	short
spurði	asked
spyr	asked
starfi	work
stenst	stood
stilla	still
sú	so
sumar	summer
sumir	some
sumum	some
svarar	answered
svo	so, such

T, t

taka	take, took
til	to, towards, until

Þ, þ

þá	then, this
það	it, that, the, this
þeir	they
þér	to-you, you
þess	this
þessa	this
þessar	this
þessu	this
þín	yours
þínar	yours
þings	assembly
þó	though
þori	dare
þrettánda	thirteenth
þrjóti	failure
þroskamaður	vigorous-man
þrýtur	ended
þú	you
því	because
þykir	think, thought

Word List (Old Icelandic to English)

Old Icelandic	English
þykja	valued

U, u

um	about
umstilli	about-guidance
ungur	young
upp	upped
uppi	up

Ú, ú

út	out-in
útferðarsaga	out-faring-saga

V, v

væri	should-be
vandi	custom
vandur	particularly
var	was
varð	was
vel	well
velkominn	welcome
ver	be
vera	be
verða	be
verr	worse
vetur	winter
við	with
vildi	willed
vilt	wish
vinnast	won
vinsæll	popular
virðast	worth
vopn	weapons

Word List *(English to Old Icelandic)*

English	Old Icelandic

A, a

about	*á, í, of, um*
about-guidance	*umstilli*
all-full	*ávallt*
allow	*heimilt*
all-well	*allvel*
also	*og*
always	*ávallt*
am	*em*
and	*að, og*
answered	*svarar*
any	*nokkverja*
are	*er, eru*
as	*er, sem*
as-a	*að*
asked	*biður, spurði, spyr*
assembly	*þings*
assistance	*ásjá*
awhile	*hríð*

B, b

be	*ver, vera, verða*
because	*því*
bid	*bað, bæði, beiðst*
boldness	*djörfung*
bore	*barst*
bright	*frálegur*
but	*eða, en*

C, c

came	*kom, koma*
clothes	*klæði*
concluded	*hætta*
could	*kunna, mun*
country	*landinu*
custom	*vandi*

D, d

dare	*þori*
did	*gerir*
discussed	*ræða*
drinking	*drekka, drykkjur*

E, e

each	*hvergi, hvert*
earlier	*áður*
ended	*lokið, þrýtur*
entertain	*skemmta*
entertained	*skemmt*
entertainment	*skemmtan*
equal	*jafnt*
equal-long	*jafndrjúg*
evening	*kveld*
everyone	*hverjum*
extraordinary	*kynlegt*

F, f

failure	*þrjóti*
find	*finna*
for-him	*sér*
for-knowing	*forvitni*
forwards	*fram*
from	*að, fram*

G, g

gave	*fékk, gefa, gefur*
gifted	*gæfu*
good	*góðan*
guess	*get, geta, getur*

Word List (English to Old Icelandic)

English	*Old Icelandic*	English	*Old Icelandic*
H, h		**M, m**	
had	*hefur*	man	*maður*
Halldor (name)	*halldóri*	many	*margir*
hand	*hönd*	may-be	*má*
has	*hefir*	me	*mér*
have	*hefir*	men	*menn*
he	*hann*	mine	*minn*
hear	*heyra*	mood	*mislyndi*
here	*hér*	most	*mest*
him	*hann, honum*	much	*miklar*
his	*sé, sína*		
how-so	*hversu*	**N, n**	
I, i		neither	*hvergi*
		none	*ekki*
I	*eg, mér*	not	*eigi, ekki*
Icelander	*íslending, íslendingur, íslenskur*	now	*nú*
if	*ef*	**O, o**	
ill	*illa, illt*		
in	*í*	of	*að, af, er, of*
is	*er*	one	*ein, einn, eitthvert*
it	*það*	or	*eða*
		out-faring-saga	*útferðarsaga*
K, k		out-in	*út*
king's-men	*hirðina*	**P, p**	
knew-of	*kynni*		
know	*kunnir*	particularly	*vandur*
		passed	*líður*
L, l		popular	*vinsæll*
less	*minna*	**R, r**	
let	*lést*		
liked	*líkar*	reason	*gegndi*
listen	*hlýtt*	recalled	*muni*
listening-to	*hlýða*	remaining	*eftir*
lord	*herra*		

Word List (English to Old Icelandic)

English	*Old Icelandic*

S, s

saga	*sagan, sögu, sögunni*
said	*kvað, sagan, sagði, segir, segja*
say	*segir, segja, sögur*
scared	*hræddur*
shall	*mun, muntu, skal*
shall-you	*skaltu*
short	*skömmum, spöl*
should	*skyldur*
should-be	*væri*
sitting	*sitja*
Snorrason (name)	*snorrasyni*
so	*sú, svo*
some	*sumir, sumum*
something	*nakkvað, nokkvern*
soon	*brátt*
spoke	*mælti*
still	*stilla*
stood	*stenst*
stories	*sögur*
such	*svo*
summer	*sumar*

T, t

take	*taka*
taught	*kenndi*
than	*en*
that	*að, en, er, það*
the	*á, að, er, hið, það*
the-day	*daginn*
the-Icelander	*íslendingur*
the-king	*konungi, konungs, konungur*
the-king's	*konungs*
the-matter	*efni*
the-men	*menn*
then	*þá*
the-saga	*sagan, söguna, sögunni*
they	*þeir*
they-are	*eru*

English	*Old Icelandic*
think	*þykir*
thirteenth	*þrettánda*
this	*að, þá, það, þess, þessa, þessar, þessu*
though	*þó*
thought	*þykir*
to	*á, að, í, til*
to-him	*honum*
to-me	*mér*
took	*nam, taka*
towards	*til*
to-you	*þér*
travelled	*fór*

U, u

un-glad	*ógleður*
until	*til*
up	*uppi*
upped	*upp*

V, v

valued	*þykja*
vigorous-man	*þroskamaður*

W, w

wares	*kaupeyri*
was	*er, eru, var, varð*
weapons	*vopn*
welcome	*velkominn*
well	*vel*
went	*fer*
what	*hví*
when	*er*
whether	*hvort*
while	*meðan*
who	*hver, sem*
willed	*vildi*
winter	*vetur*
wisdom	*fræði*
wish	*vilt*

Word List (English to Old Icelandic)

English	*Old Icelandic*
with	*með, við*
won	*vinnast*
work	*starfi*
worse	*verr*
worth	*virðast*
would	*mun, muni*

Y, y

you	*þér, þú*
young	*ungur*
yours	*þín, þínar*
yule	*jóla, jólanna, jólin, jólunum*
yule-day	*jóladag*

A Word Comparison of Old Norse and Old Icelandic Words

Old Norse	Old Icelandic	English	Old Norse	Old Icelandic	English
áðr	áður	earlier	skyldr	skyldur	should
at	að	and	spyrr	spyr	asked
at	að	as-a	stenzt	stenst	stood
at	að	from	svá	svo	so
at	að	of	svá	svo	such
at	að	that	þat	það	it
at	að	the	þat	það	that
at	að	this	þat	það	the
at	að	to	þat	það	this
beiðzt	beiðst	bid	þroskamaðr	þroskamaður	vigorous-man
biðr	biður	asked	þrýtr	þrýtur	ended
ek	eg	I	þykkir	þykir	think
fekk	fékk	gave	þykkir	þykir	thought
Ferr	fer	went	þykkja	þykja	valued
fráligr	frálegur	bright	ungr	ungur	young
gefr	gefur	gave	vanði	vandi	custom
getr	getur	guess	vandr	vandur	particularly
hefr	hefur	had	vápn	vopn	weapons
Hræddr	hræddur	scared	vetr	vetur	winter
hvárt	hvort	whether	vill	vilt	wish
hverr	hver	who			
hverrgi	hvergi	each			
líðr	líður	passed			
Íslendingr	íslendingur	Icelander			
Íslendingr	íslendingur	the-Icelander			
íslenzkr	íslenskur	Icelander			
it	hið	the			
Konungr	konungur	the-king			
kynligt	kynlegt	extraordinary			
lézt	lést	let			
lokit	lokið	ended			
maðr	maður	man			
namk	nam	took			
nökkura	nokkverja	any			
nökkurn	nokkvern	something			
nökkut	nakkvað	something			
ógleðr	ógleður	un-glad			
ok	og	also			
ok	og	and			

www.ingramcontent.com/pod-product-compliance
Lightning Source LLC
Chambersburg PA
CBHW051432070526
44584CB00023B/3686